This book belongs to...

*For Fenya and Ozra, may you grow into a world
where these beautiful creatures reign. - J.S.*

*To all those who look after our planet,
and all the miraculous animals on it. - B.K.*

Published in 2024 by Welbeck Editions
An Imprint of Hachette Children's Books,
Part of Hodder & Stoughton Limited
Carmelite House, 50 Victoria Embankment
London EC4Y 0DZ

An Hachette UK Company
www.hachette.co.uk
www.hachettechildrens.co.uk

Design and layout © Hachette Children's Books 2024
Text © 2024 Jess French
Illustration © 2024 Brendan Kearney
Jess French and Brendan Kearney have asserted their moral
rights to be identified as the author and illustrator of this Work
in accordance with the Copyright Designs and Patents Act 1988.

ISBN 978 1 80338 171 8

Printed in China
10 9 8 7 6 5 4 3 2 1

MIX
Paper | Supporting
responsible forestry
FSC® C020056
FSC
www.fsc.org

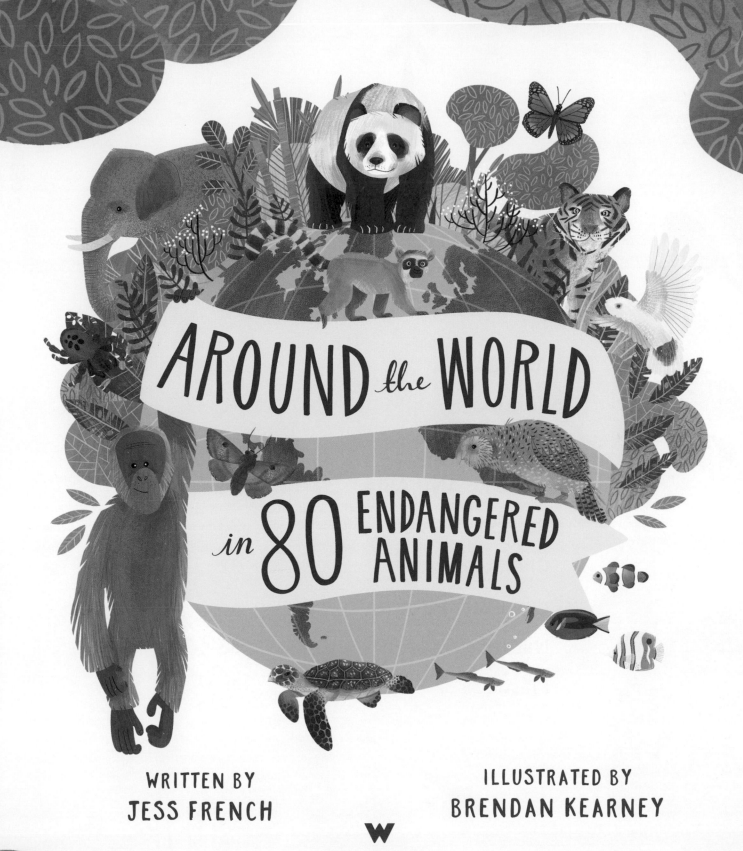

AROUND the WORLD
in 80 ENDANGERED ANIMALS

WRITTEN BY
JESS FRENCH

ILLUSTRATED BY
BRENDAN KEARNEY

W
WELBECK
EDITIONS

CONTENTS

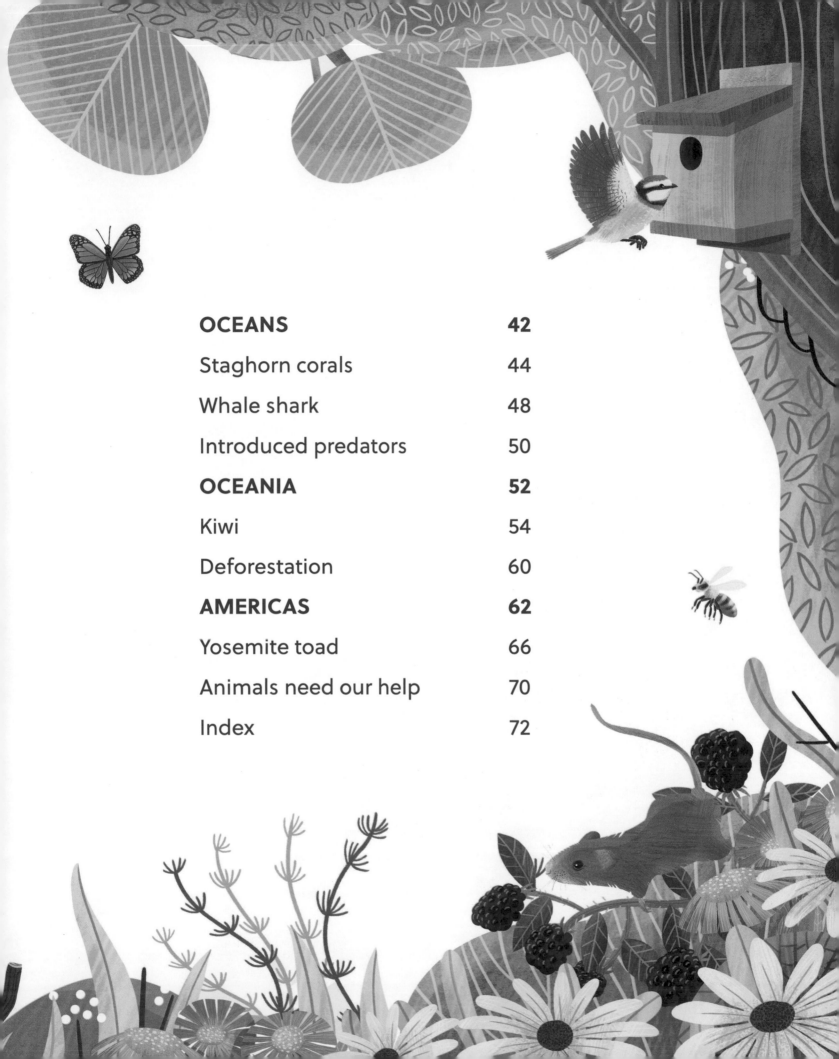

OUR WORLD of AMAZING ANIMALS

Aren't we lucky to live in a world that is bursting with so many extraordinary animals?

From the tiny scuttlers to the soaring giants, animals can be found in every corner of our planet—and they are full of fascinating surprises. Sadly, not all animals are thriving. Human actions are making life tough for some creatures.

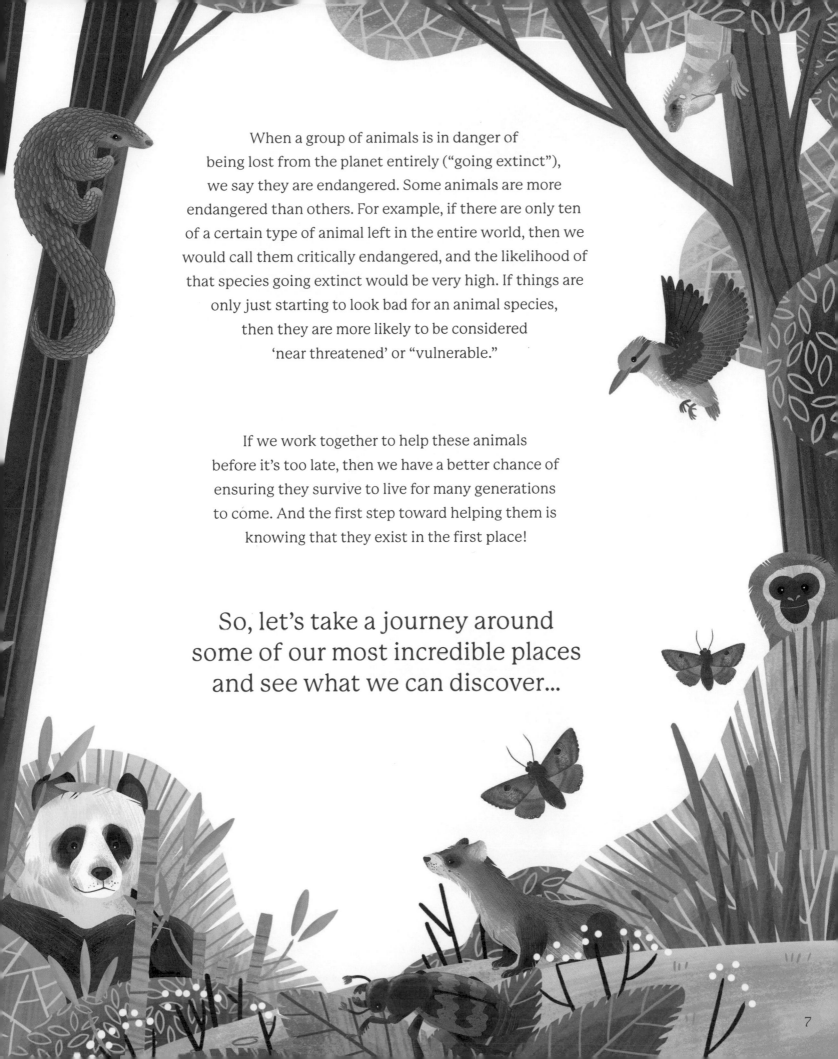

When a group of animals is in danger of
being lost from the planet entirely ("going extinct"),
we say they are endangered. Some animals are more
endangered than others. For example, if there are only ten
of a certain type of animal left in the entire world, then we
would call them critically endangered, and the likelihood of
that species going extinct would be very high. If things are
only just starting to look bad for an animal species,
then they are more likely to be considered
'near threatened' or "vulnerable."

If we work together to help these animals
before it's too late, then we have a better chance of
ensuring they survive to live for many generations
to come. And the first step toward helping them is
knowing that they exist in the first place!

So, let's take a journey around
some of our most incredible places
and see what we can discover...

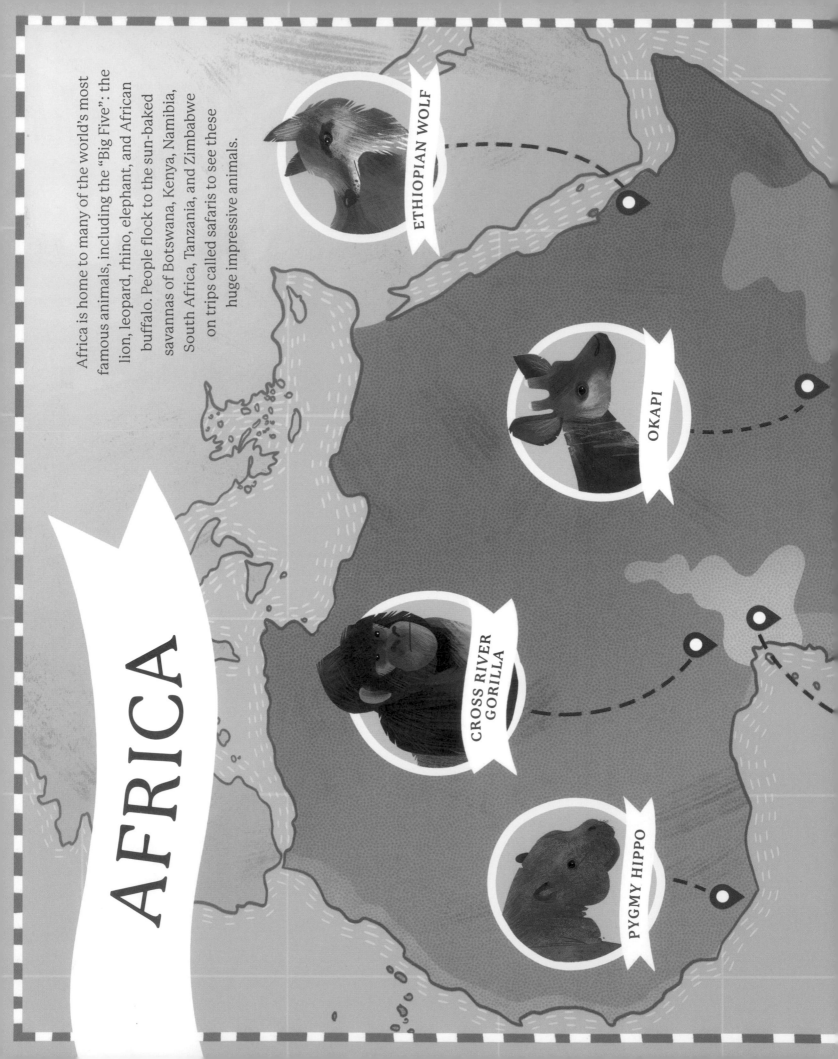

AFRICA

Africa is home to many of the world's most famous animals, including the "Big Five": the lion, leopard, rhino, elephant, and African buffalo. People flock to the sun-baked savannas of Botswana, Kenya, Namibia, South Africa, Tanzania, and Zimbabwe on trips called safaris to see these huge impressive animals.

ETHIOPIAN WOLF

OKAPI

CROSS RIVER GORILLA

PYGMY HIPPO

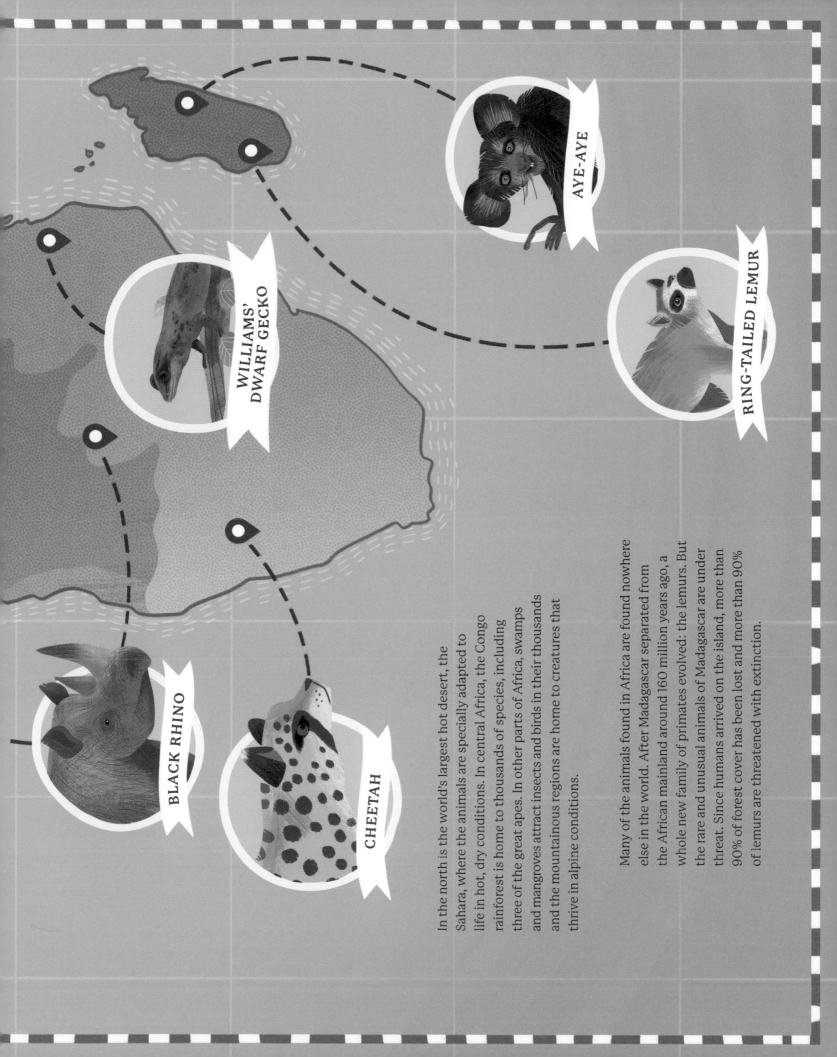

AYE-AYE

WILLIAMS' DWARF GECKO

RING-TAILED LEMUR

BLACK RHINO

CHEETAH

In the north is the world's largest hot desert, the Sahara, where the animals are specially adapted to life in hot, dry conditions. In central Africa, the Congo rainforest is home to thousands of species, including three of the great apes. In other parts of Africa, swamps and mangroves attract insects and birds in their thousands and the mountainous regions are home to creatures that thrive in alpine conditions.

Many of the animals found in Africa are found nowhere else in the world. After Madagascar separated from the African mainland around 160 million years ago, a whole new family of primates evolved: the lemurs. But the rare and unusual animals of Madagascar are under threat. Since humans arrived on the island, more than 90% of forest cover has been lost and more than 90% of lemurs are threatened with extinction.

1. Black rhino

On a hot, sunny day, the best place to find a rhino is at the wallows. Rhinos love nothing better than rolling around in the cool, wet earth, covering themselves in a thick layer of sunproof mud. Even without the mud, rhinos are funny-looking. Their huge bodies are covered in leathery gray skin, which crinkles at the creases, like a baggy, oversized coat! Rhinos have incredible horns, made of keratin—the same material that makes up our fingernails and hair. Sadly, people can sell these horns for lots of money, so the biggest threat to rhinos is people hunting them.

2. Addax

With possibly the best set of headgear in the Sahara, the addax antelope makes quite an impression as it strides through the African desert. It is perfectly adapted to life in hot and dry weather. Its pale coat reflects sunlight, its broad, flat feet stop it from sinking into the sand, and its ability to survive without water for long periods of time allow it to survive periods of drought.

3. Secretary bird

Stomp, stomp, kick! That's the sound of a secretary bird stamping on the head of a snake— its favorite method of hunting. Unusually for a bird, the long-legged secretary bird hunts on the ground, strutting through the shrub and grasslands of sub-Saharan Africa like an eagle on stilts.

4. Ethiopian wolf

The soft, orange fur and brushlike tail of the Ethiopian wolf are a lot like those of its cousin, the fox. Like foxes, Ethiopian wolves are part of the canid family, which also contains domestic dogs and other wolves. Ethiopian wolves are the rarest members of the canid family and they are still threatened by habitat loss and diseases that they can catch from pet dogs. It is thought there are less than 500 Ethiopian wolves left in the wild and they are only found in the mountains of Ethiopia.

5. Grevy's zebra

In the heart of the African savanna, a creature approaches at speed. Through a cloud of dust, it is only possible to catch snatches of the animal: a thunder of hooves, a flash of stripes, a bray and a snort. Then its horselike features come into clearer focus—it can only be a zebra! Of the three species of zebra, the Grevy's zebra is the largest and rarest. Its survival is closely linked to the protection of its grasslands.

6. Cheetah

Whooooosh! Accelerating from 0-37mph in only three seconds, just by taking three enormous strides, the cheetah is the fastest land animal on Earth. It zooms across African grasslands, hunting down animals such as antelopes, birds, and hares.

Cheetahs prefer to hunt during the day to reduce the risk of their prey being stolen by lions or hyenas.

7. Bonobo

A group of slender, dark-haired apes lounge in a fruit tree, sharing their fruit, flowers, and leaves. These are bonobos, the apes that are most famous for being peacemakers.

Bonobos look very similar to their larger cousins, chimpanzees, and both species live very close to one another in the Democratic Republic of the Congo. But anyone taking the time to watch a group of bonobos would soon realize that the two kinds of ape are very different in nature. Least aggressive of all the apes, bonobos are more likely to be seen hugging than fighting. They live in large groups led by females and are very kind and caring towards one another.

Bonobos are only found in a small area and very little of their home range is protected, so bonobos are threatened by hunting, deforestation, and human fighting. As we are so closely related, humans can also pass infectious diseases to bonobos which can make them very unwell.

Bonobos often live in large groups, though some of the group members may go off and do their own thing from time to time. They come together again at night, to make cozy nests up in the trees.

8. Gorilla

Gorillas are the largest of the great apes. They have broad chests and muscular shoulders, which can make them appear very frightening. In reality, gorillas are gentle giants who spend most of their time quietly munching on leaves. There are four subspecies of gorilla, of which the Cross River gorilla is the rarest.

9. Chimpanzee

Unlike the peaceful bonobo, chimpanzee groups are ruled by males, who use aggression instead of peace to get their way. Like us, chimpanzees use tools, communicate with one another, make friends, and even wage wars. They are found across western and central Africa, where they live in the forests eating fruits and plants, and sometimes hunting other animals.

10. Aye-aye

In the forests of Madagascar, under the cover of darkness, one of the world's strangest-looking animals clambers from branch to branch in search of bugs to eat. The aye-aye's whole body is perfectly designed for this task. First it taps on wood, then uses its big ears to listen for movement within, and finally uses its long middle finger to pull out what it has heard and gobbles it up—yum!

11. Tanzania screeching frog

Most frogs lay eggs in water, which hatch out into tadpoles that metamorphose into frogs. Not the Tanzania screeching frog! These small frogs spend their lives hopping about in the leaf litter before laying eggs on land, which hatch into tiny little versions of themselves. Weird!

12. Seychelles forest scorpion

The Seychelles are home to all kinds of extraordinary animals which are not found anywhere else in the world, such as the Seychelles forest scorpion. Now found only on one island—Silhouette Island—the Seychelles forest scorpion is one of the rarest scorpions in the world. They are very caring mothers, carrying their young on their backs until the babies are old enough to look after themselves.

13. Ring-tailed lemur

In Madagascar, lemurs rule. There are more than 100 different species and they come in all shapes and sizes—the ring-tailed lemur is probably the most famous. The lemur family is the most endangered group of all vertebrates, with 98% of lemurs threatened with extinction.

Males fight by using a scent gland in their bottoms that puts a smell on their tails, which they then wave at each other. Stinky!

14. Pygmy hippo

Unlike their giant, extrovert cousins, pygmy hippos prefer a quiet life, hidden away in the swamps and forest of west Africa. They come out to munch on plants once the temperature drops in the late afternoon, and will continue chomping well into the night!

15. Okapi

The okapi's closest relative is a famous long-necked mammal! In fact, the okapi is often known as the "forest giraffe"—but it looks more like a cross between a zebra and a deer. Its unusual coloring helps it to move unseen through dense forests, using its long, flexible tongue to strip leaves from branches as it goes.

16. Algerian nuthatch

In Algeria's mountain forests, Algerian nuthatches clamber up and down the trunks of trees, searching for bugs in the bark. Nuthatches are found all over the world, but the Algerian nuthatch is found only in north Africa.

17. African wild dog

The African wild dog is one of the most endangered animals in the whole of Africa. These beautiful carnivores are also known as African painted dogs due to the patches on their coats – every wild dog has its own unique pattern. These wild dogs hunt in packs, and when to hunt is a group decision. They vote by sneezing – the more sneezes, the more likely it is they'll go hunting.

18. Williams' dwarf gecko

The electric blue Williams' dwarf gecko is only found in one place in the wild: the Kimboza forest in Tanzania. Unfortunately, its beautiful color has made it popular in the pet trade and collectors frequently capture Williams' dwarf geckos from the wild to be sold as pets.

19. Albany adder

There have only been around thirty sightings of South Africa's rare Albany adder since it was first discovered in 1937. In fact, it is so rare that conservationists are keeping the Albany adders' location a secret, in case anyone tries to steal them.

EXTINCTION

We all know that animals go extinct.

If they didn't, we might see stegosauruses wandering
down our streets or pterodactyls soaring past our windows.
The Earth has changed a lot since the first animals appeared—oceans
and mountains have come and gone; continents have broken apart.
The world we live in now is not the same world that existed hundreds
of millions of years ago, so it's understandable that the animals
that live on Earth now are different too.

In fact, animals are still going extinct all the time. If that's totally normal, then why are we worried about extinction? The problem we are facing is the *rate* of extinction. Normally, animals go extinct gradually. A few species that are not well suited to their environment disappear and they are replaced by new, better-adapted animals. That's not what is happening now. Right now, we are in the middle of a *mass extinction*. During a mass extinction, up to 95% of all animals can be lost. The last one happened around 65 million years ago—when the dinosaurs were wiped out. The other thing that is unusual about what's happening right now is that it's *all because of us*. And we humans are the ones who have the power to stop it.

There is no single thing that humans are doing to cause so many creatures to become extinct. Pollution, overfishing, deforestation, global warming, and the introduction of predators to new habitats are all contributing to the rapid decline of animals around the world. The good thing is, knowing the cause of these extinctions can help us to stop them.

LADYBIRD SPIDER

MALLORCAN
MIDWIFE TOAD

EUROPEAN
HAMSTER

SNOW LEOPARD

MADEIRAN
LAND SNAIL

DHOLE

EUROPE

AND ASIA

ASIAN ELEPHANT

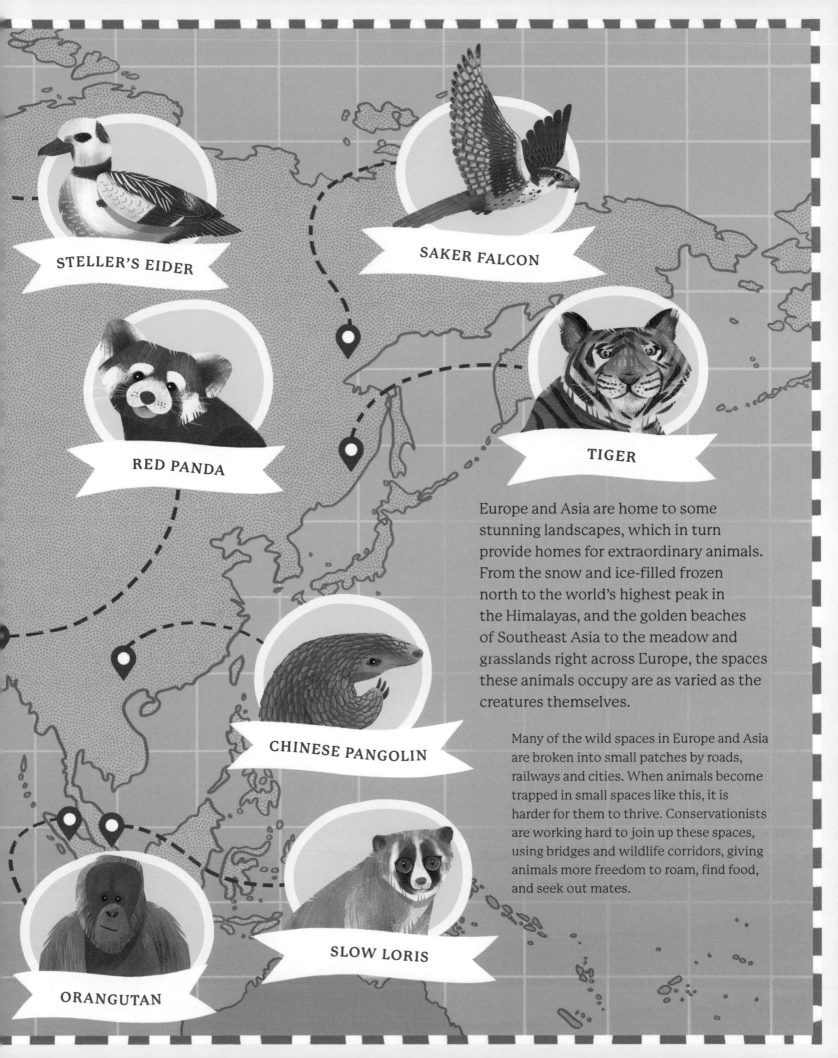

STELLER'S EIDER

SAKER FALCON

RED PANDA

TIGER

CHINESE PANGOLIN

SLOW LORIS

ORANGUTAN

Europe and Asia are home to some stunning landscapes, which in turn provide homes for extraordinary animals. From the snow and ice-filled frozen north to the world's highest peak in the Himalayas, and the golden beaches of Southeast Asia to the meadow and grasslands right across Europe, the spaces these animals occupy are as varied as the creatures themselves.

Many of the wild spaces in Europe and Asia are broken into small patches by roads, railways and cities. When animals become trapped in small spaces like this, it is harder for them to thrive. Conservationists are working hard to join up these spaces, using bridges and wildlife corridors, giving animals more freedom to roam, find food, and seek out mates.

20. Red panda

A vibrant coat of red fur, bright, inquisitive eyes, and a long, bushy tail are the trademarks of this small, bamboo-munching mammal. The red panda is an excellent climber, moving expertly through the branches in search of food. It lives in chilly mountain forests, where its dense, fluffy fur protects it from the cold.

21. Snow leopard

Prowling on huge, padded paws, the majestic and secretive snow leopard slinks silently through snowy landscapes. This elusive big cat is so well camouflaged that it can be almost impossible to see—even if you are close by. Scientists studying snow leopards must be very patient! They often have to climb high up mountains and wait for long periods of time in the cold, relying on camera traps and their tracking skills to get the answers they are looking for.

22. Tiger

It's easy to recognize a tiger by its fiery orange stripes, but this distinctive coloring also helps it to creep unseen through grasslands and forests. Once found across Asia, for many years tigers and people struggled to live side-by-side and tiger numbers dropped rapidly. Happily, in the last few years there are signs that tiger populations are beginning to recover—now it's more important than ever to protect their homes and keep the remaining tigers safe.

23. Orangutan

In the forests of Borneo and Sumatra, our shaggy orange cousins, the orangutans, swing through the trees. We once thought there were only two species of orangutan, but in 2017 a new species was discovered! Named the Tapanuli orangutan, it brought the total number of orangutan species to three.

24. Hainan gibbon

Orangutans are not the only apes swinging through the forests of Asia. Though they look a bit like tailless monkeys, gibbons are apes too. There are around 20 species of gibbon, including the critically endangered Hainan gibbon. Conservationists are working hard to save the Hainan gibbon, but with fewer than 30 individuals left in the wild, the race is on to save the world's rarest primate before it goes extinct.

25. Slow loris

As night falls in the cloud forests of Java, the slow loris uses lianas and vines to make a steady path through the trees. Its huge eyes, small round ears, and soft, fluffy body gives the slow loris *major* cute factor. But its sweet appearance hides a surprising secret—special glands on the slow loris' arms ooze a nasty toxin, which it rubs onto its mouth, giving it a venomous bite.

26. Chinese Pangolin

Like a cross between an anteater, a woodlouse, and a lizard, pangolins are scaly, insect-eating mammals that roll up into balls when they are frightened. They are odd-looking creatures, with small heads and long tongues, thick, strong tails, and huge claws for breaking into ants' nests.

There are eight different species of pangolin, four that live in Africa and four that live in Asia. All of them are endangered by humans, who kill pangolins for their meat and scales. Despite being covered in a scaly coat of armor, pangolins have little to protect them from humans, who can easily scoop them up and carry them away. Combined with the popularity of their scales in traditional Chinese medicine, this has led to pangolins being given the unfortunate title of "most trafficked animal in the world."

27. Panda

Their huge fluffy bodies, cute round faces, and funny, clumsy movements have won the hearts of people all over the globe, but despite their fame, life hasn't always been smooth sailing for the giant panda. Giant pandas were once the most famous endangered animals in the whole world, and the story of the black-and-white bear who feeds only on bamboo was once the first thing that popped into people's minds when they thought about conservation and the threat of extinction. In the 1970s there were only 1,114 wild pandas left in China and unless serious action was taken, it looked like they might disappear entirely.

Luckily, the world did wake up to the plight of the panda and panda numbers have been rising steadily ever since. There are now nearly 70 giant panda nature reserves across China and there are at least 1,864 giant pandas living in the wild.

28. Ladybird spider

Is it a ladybird? Is it a spider? No, it's a ladybug (also called a ladybird) spider! These cute little arachnids spend most of their time in cozy silk-lined burrows, only emerging to catch food and mate. Much of their natural habitat has been destroyed but luckily they have been given a helping hand by conservationists, who transport them safely to their new homes inside empty water bottles.

29. Iberian lynx

With its short tail, tufted ears, and majestic beard, the Iberian lynx should be easy to identify but it is a master of disguise! When stalking its way through shrubby mountain regions, the Iberian lynx is nearly impossible to see—bad news for the rabbits and partridge it preys upon. Iberian lynx numbers have grown rapidly in the last decade, but despite this it is still one of the most endangered cats on the planet.

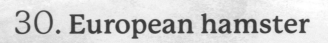

30. European hamster

European hamsters may be small, but they are feisty! Found in grasslands throughout central Europe, they can also be seen in cities, shoveling human leftovers into their elastic cheek pouches. If you see one, watch out—they have been known to leap into the air to nip unsuspecting fingers if you get too close!

31. Mallorcan midwife toad

After laying their spawn, most toads leave their eggs to fend for themselves. Not Mallorcan midwife toads, though! The male Mallorcan midwife toad carefully wraps the string of fertilized eggs around his legs and back, carrying them with him until they are ready to hatch.

32. Saker falcon

We often think of falcons as small, delicate birds, but not the Saker falcon. It is huge and powerful, with wings stretching over three feet across. Like most falcons, the saker is an aerial acrobat, shooting through the air at speeds of up to 200mph. Saker falcons are found across Africa, Asia, and Europe. In Middle Eastern countries they are commonly kept as pets.

33. Steller's eider

When you picture the Arctic, the first bird that comes to mind probably isn't a duck, but that's exactly where the beautiful Steller's eider makes its home. Often nesting beside icy lakes, the female Steller's eider packs her nest with bits of plant and fluffy down feathers to keep her eggs toasty and warm.

34. Madeiran land snail

At only 0.04 inch long, Madeiran land snails are easily overlooked. Luckily for them, conservationists realized that without a serious international conservation effort, these tiny snails were soon going to go extinct. Teams from the UK and Portugal jumped to action, bringing the snails into captivity to breed.

35. Komodo dragon

If dragons really did exist, they probably wouldn't look too different from the Komodo dragon. Komodo dragons don't have wings or breathe fire, but they are huge, scaly predators that strike awe and wonder into the hearts of those that they meet.

The curved, serrated teeth of the Komodo dragon are more similar to those of sharks than other lizards and they have a venomous bite, which prevents wounds from healing and reduces blood pressure.

Komodo dragons are the biggest and heaviest of all the lizards and have an appetite to match! They are not fussy eaters; they will eat animals that have already died or hunt food down themselves. They are ambush hunters, often spending long periods hidden in the undergrowth, waiting for a suitable victim to pass by.

Komodo dragons are only found on the Lesser Sunda Islands of Indonesia, which are threatened by rising sea levels. If humans don't change their actions soon, up to 71% of Komodo dragon habitat could slip beneath the waves in the next 45 years.

36. Chinese giant salamander

Its bulbous head and long, flattened tail make the Chinese giant salamander look like a giant tadpole with legs! It is the biggest amphibian in the world, reaching lengths of up to 6 feet. It spends most of its life underwater, living and breeding in large hill streams in the forests of China, but it is threatened by hunting, as its meat is considered a delicacy in some countries.

37. Gharial

The extraordinary gharial is impossible to confuse with any other kind of crocodile. Its long, thin snout may not look practical but it's perfect for snapping up fish—its favorite prey! Gharials are found in small populations in northern India and Nepal, but they are very shy and will usually run away as soon as they see people.

38. Saola

The mysterious saola was only discovered in 1992 and remains one of the world's rarest large mammals. Though it looks a lot like an antelope, the saola is actually more closely related to wild cattle and buffaloes. It is only found in the remote jungle of the Annamite mountain range.

39. Red-vented cockatoo

Red-vented cockatoos were once found in big, noisy flocks in mangroves and forests across the Philippines. Now they are restricted to the Palawan islands, where they are still threatened with habitat loss and collection for the exotic pet trade.

40. Asian elephant

Asian elephants are smaller than their African cousins, but they are still the biggest land animals in all of Asia. They live in herds, stomping through broadleaf forests all the way across the continent in search of shrubs and other leafy plants to eat. Sadly, their homes are rapidly being destroyed and replaced with farms, mines, and roads.

41. Dhole

An eerie whistling sound is carried on the wind through the hilly forests of eastern and southern Asia. Is it a bird? An insect? Perhaps a monkey? The noise made by the dhole, also known as the whistling dog, is not what you would expect from an athletic carnivore. Dhole packs use an impressive array of sounds, from whistles and clicks to high-pitched screams, to communicate between themselves and coordinate their attacks on prey.

42. Honey bee

Bees may be small, but they are mighty! We owe a lot to these little buzzing insects. Not only do honey bees provide us with delicious sweet honey to put on our toast, they also pollinate many of the plants that provide us with fruits, vegetables, and nuts to eat. Without bees, our plates would look very different! It is important that, in return, we make sure to plant lots of bee-friendly plants, so the bees can keep their energy levels up while doing their important work.

CLIMATE CHANGE

Feeling hot, hot, hot?

That's no surprise, as our planet is rapidly heating up. Since we humans started burning fossil fuels such as oil, coal, and gas on a large scale, the world's temperatures have been rising. Ice caps are melting, extreme weather events are becoming more common, and people are being forced to leave their homes— we call this global warming.

Scientists first realized that the burning of fossil fuels affected our climate in the early 1980s. They found a link between certain gases in the atmosphere and a change in global weather. Now we know that these gases form an insulating layer in the atmosphere and prevent heat from leaving.

Heat energy from the Sun travels through the atmosphere and heats up the surface of the Earth.

Heat energy travels through the atmosphere back out into space.

Atmosphere

Some of this energy is absorbed and some is reflected. Ice and snow reflect a lot of heat energy.

Carbon dioxide and methane, among other gases, make it harder for heat energy to pass back out, so more heat is trapped inside the atmosphere. This causes the temperature of the Earth to rise.

For some animals, even a change of a couple of degrees can make certain environments unliveable. If plants fail to grow because the temperature no longer suits them, then all of the animals that rely on that plant to eat will die out too. Some environments, like the polar ice sheets, are disappearing altogether because of global warming.

NATURE'S WORKERS

Every species on Earth has an important job to perform. Nature has created a delicate balance that keeps our beautiful planet healthy and full of all sorts of amazing life. We cannot afford to lose any of these hard-working creatures. Our home depends on them—and so do we!

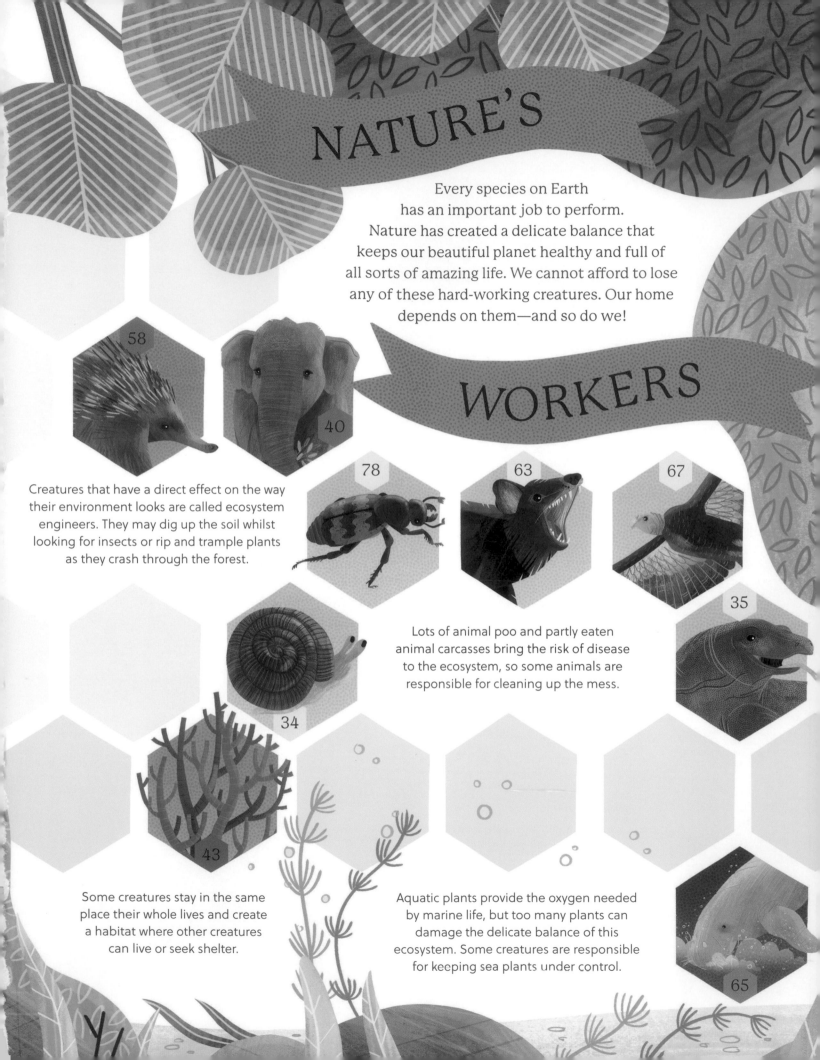

58

40

78

63

67

35

Creatures that have a direct effect on the way their environment looks are called ecosystem engineers. They may dig up the soil whilst looking for insects or rip and trample plants as they crash through the forest.

Lots of animal poo and partly eaten animal carcasses bring the risk of disease to the ecosystem, so some animals are responsible for cleaning up the mess.

34

43

Some creatures stay in the same place their whole lives and create a habitat where other creatures can live or seek shelter.

Aquatic plants provide the oxygen needed by marine life, but too many plants can damage the delicate balance of this ecosystem. Some creatures are responsible for keeping sea plants under control.

65

Some animals help new plants to grow by gobbling their fruits and carrying their seeds to new locations. These plant-eaters produce poo which is rich in nutrients and works as an excellent fertiliser.

Many plants rely on pollinators to help them to produce new, healthy seeds. The pollinators will visit hundreds of flowers each day. Pollinators are also vital for growing the crops which are needed to feed the world's human population.

WHAT IS

Our incredible world
is bursting with life—from
tiny bacteria to towering trees,
it's what makes our planet so
special. The variety of living things
that exists in an area is called its
"biodiversity"—and it's a
kind of superpower!

BIODIVERSITY?

*Turn the page to learn more
about how the animals in this book
keep our planet healthy.*

Why is it so important?

We all rely on one another to survive and thrive. An ecosystem is a community of living things that are found within a specific area. Within every ecosystem there are many different living things, each with their own role to play. There are recyclers, producers, scavengers, and builders and all of them work together in the great web of life to keep their ecosystem running as it should. The more different living things there are within an ecosystem, the healthier that ecosystem is because it means the jobs are shared between lots more workers.

Animals that can survive on lots of different foods, known as omnivores, make their ecosystem more resistant to changes. If low rainfall means a certain plant has not grown well, omnivores can switch to eating something else, leaving the plants that remain for animals that have stricter dietary requirements.

Too many grazing animals will damage the plant life of an ecosystem, so large predators are needed to control these populations and keep the environment healthy for everyone.

Just like on land, there are large predators who control the populations of smaller marine predators. They make sure that there aren't too many of any type of creature and are essential for maintaining a natural balance.

25 53 56 30 10 23 20 41 7 9 22 29 17 21 6 4 45 50 75 49 68 36 80 37

Some creatures prey on small animals, fish, and insects to prevent those populations getting too big and damaging the environment.

Filter-feeders are some of the largest creatures on Earth. They feed on plankton—tiny organisms that float on the ocean currents like a nutritious soup—and play an important role in controlling the populations of many freshwater and ocean creatures.

These creatures feed on small fish, crustaceans or insects, controlling those populations and making sure there are not too many for the ecosystem to support.

PLASTIC

Plastic is amazing, isn't it?

Lightweight, strong, easily molded into all manner of shapes, and relatively cheap to produce. Before plastic was invented, all of the materials used by people were natural: wood, stone, bone, tusk, horn. Plastics soon provided alternatives for almost all of these— and plastics were considered extremely environmentally friendly, as they stopped people from having to use up natural materials. Back then, we didn't know what the long-term effects of using so much plastic would be on the planet.

Soon, we became obsessed with plastic—and it's easy to see why. But there is a dark side to this plastic revolution. Plastics are often made from fossil fuels such as oil and natural gas, and fossil fuels are often burned to make them. While making plastic is pretty easy, disposing of it can be very difficult. Unlike natural materials, which our clever planet can break down and recycle, plastic takes a long time to degrade—and even when it does, it only turns into smaller pieces of plastic, which can easily be swallowed by animals.

Many of the plastic items we use in our day-to-day lives are used just once before being thrown away. Plastic waste suffocates, traps, injures, and poisons animals all over the planet, especially in our oceans. Soon there will be more pieces of plastic in the ocean than fish. If we want a decent future for our world's incredible creatures, then we cannot keep on using plastic at the rate we are right now. We need to find a new way.

OCEANS

ATLANTIC COD

From above, the ocean can look calm, flat, and empty. But under the waves, oceans are bursting with life! Every salty drop swarms with tiny sea creatures. These small organisms form the base of a food chain that serves millions of others, including the biggest animal ever to have lived: the blue whale.

The ocean is not one single habitat. Within the ocean, variations in temperature, amount of light, saltiness, pressure, and depth determine which plants and animals can survive. There are areas of ocean that are so cold, fish have special proteins in their blood so they do not freeze. There are parts of the ocean so dark that the animals that live there must themselves create the light. There are places in the ocean so colorful, it's hard to believe they are not straight from the pages of a magical storybook.

STAGHORN CORALS

The ocean is enormous, covering 71% of our whole planet. But we have explored the moon more than our own ocean. There are still so many secrets to uncover in its watery depths—we have only just scratched the surface.

WHALE SHARK

SOUTHERN BLUEFIN TUNA

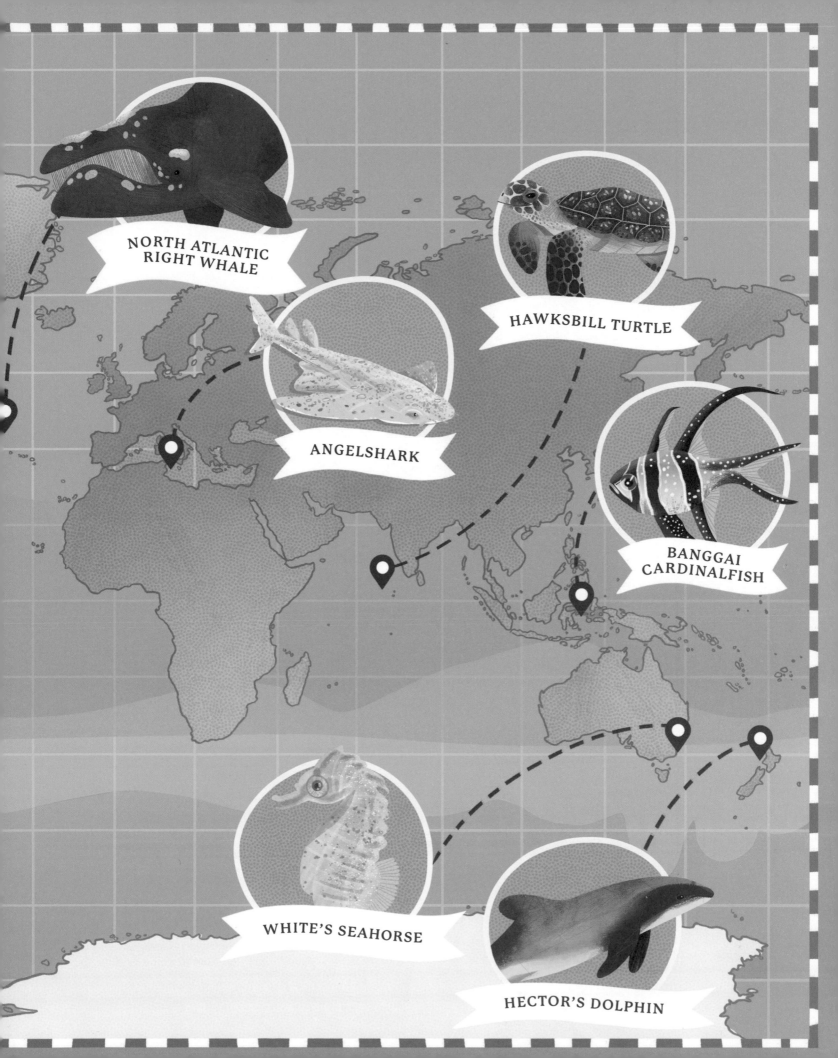

NORTH ATLANTIC
RIGHT WHALE

HAWKSBILL TURTLE

ANGELSHARK

BANGGAI
CARDINALFISH

WHITE'S SEAHORSE

HECTOR'S DOLPHIN

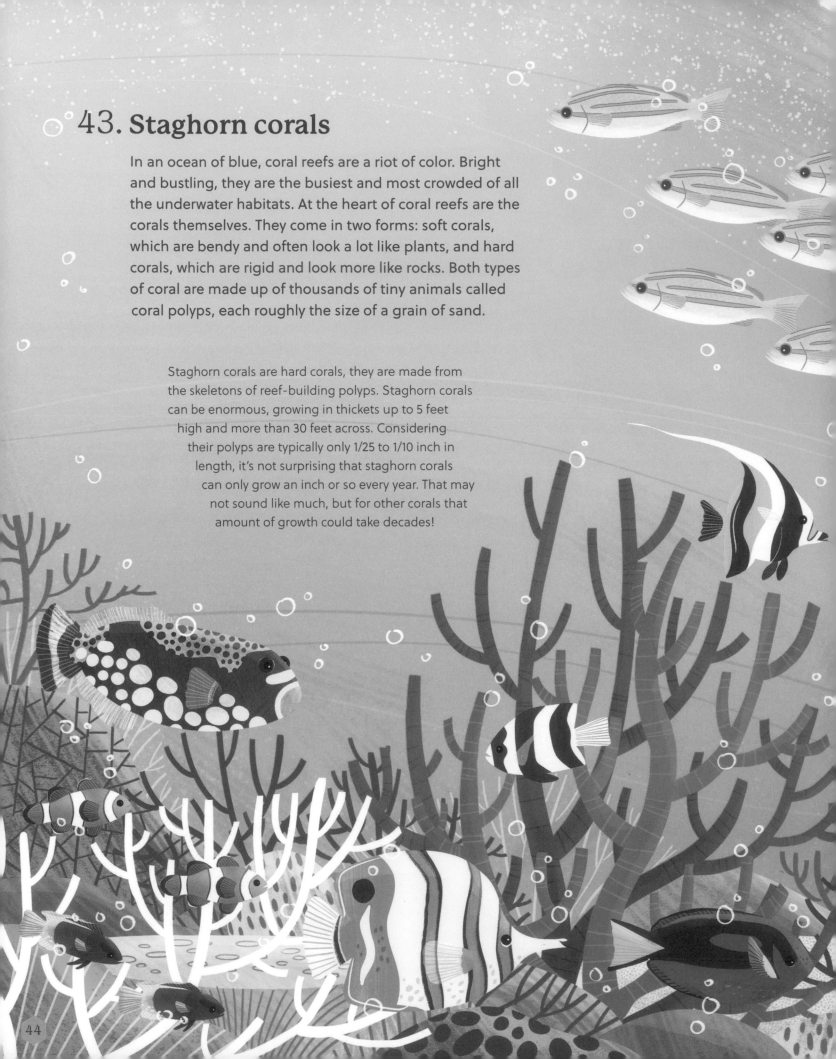

43. Staghorn corals

In an ocean of blue, coral reefs are a riot of color. Bright and bustling, they are the busiest and most crowded of all the underwater habitats. At the heart of coral reefs are the corals themselves. They come in two forms: soft corals, which are bendy and often look a lot like plants, and hard corals, which are rigid and look more like rocks. Both types of coral are made up of thousands of tiny animals called coral polyps, each roughly the size of a grain of sand.

Staghorn corals are hard corals, they are made from the skeletons of reef-building polyps. Staghorn corals can be enormous, growing in thickets up to 5 feet high and more than 30 feet across. Considering their polyps are typically only 1/25 to 1/10 inch in length, it's not surprising that staghorn corals can only grow an inch or so every year. That may not sound like much, but for other corals that amount of growth could take decades!

Known as the "rainforests of the sea." coral reefs provide shelter and protection for at least a quarter of all ocean species, despite covering just 0.1% of the ocean.

Coral reefs are gravely endangered by water pollution, disease, fishing, and—more than anything else— climate change. If we lose these vital habitats, it's possible that we would lose a quarter of all ocean species along with them.

44. Atlantic cod

There were once so many cod in the North Atlantic Ocean that Cape Cod was named in their honor. Catching Atlantic cod was easy then—the ocean was full of them! But by 1992, there were so few cod left in the waters around Newfoundland, Canada, that a ban was imposed, preventing fishers from catching them. Now, several decades later, we are much more aware of the need to limit how many fish we take from our seas.

45. Angelshark

Picture a shark! What came to mind? Probably not a flat-bodied angelshark, buried beneath the sand, waiting to ambush its dinner. Angelsharks are a type of "flat shark," critically endangered fish that look more like rays than sharks. Their habit of hanging out on the ocean floor makes them very vulnerable to any fishing practices which scrape nets along the seabed.

46. North Atlantic right whale

Right whales are baleen whales, part of the same family as blue and humpback whales. Like all the gentle giants in their family, right whales have plates called baleen instead of teeth, which allow them to filter krill, plankton, and small fish from the water to eat. The name "right whale" comes from the fact that early whalers identified them as the "right" whales to kill. Though they are no longer targeted directly, they often get caught up in fishing gear and are sometimes hit by boats.

47. Hector's dolphin

A dark fin breaks the surface...a glistening gray back soon follows. Suddenly they are everywhere, Hector's dolphins fill the water around the boat. Despite being so endangered, they are very friendly and inquisitive and pods of up to twenty individuals can be seen surfing the waves, playing with seaweed, or just getting a good look at the humans on board.

48. White's seahorse

Endangered White's seahorses off the coast of Sydney have been given a helping hand by conservationists who have built them "seahorse hotels"—places they can safely come together and breed. Eventually, the goal is for the sponges, seagrasses, and soft corals that White's seahorses once called home to return to Australia's east coast, but until then, they will be protected in their makeshift homes.

49. Southern bluefin tuna

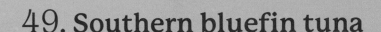

Sharks and killer whales are not the only predators cruising the open oceans...tuna are large, strong, streamlined hunters which can shoot speedily through the water like silvery torpedoes when chasing their prey. These marine super-athletes can also dive deep down into icy waters and hunt in packs like lions. Amazing!

50. Hawksbill turtle

Our oceans are home to seven majestic species of sea turtle: large ocean reptiles which can be found gliding through tropical waters, only coming to land to lay their eggs. The beautiful hawksbill turtle is one of the rarest. Most often found in coral reefs, it pokes around in nooks and crevices, using its pointed beak to pry out sponges to eat.

51. Banggai cardinalfish

In the wild, the uniquely patterned Banggai cardinalfish is only found in the waters around the Banggai archipelago, but in fish tanks, it is found all over the world. It is really important that we stop taking fish from the ocean to keep as pets and start protecting their natural habitats if we want them to survive in the wild.

52. Whale shark

A huge and majestic creature moves slowly through the brilliant blue water, its vast mouth held wide to capture plankton and small fish. It would be easy to mistake this animal for a whale, but it's actually the world's largest fish: the whale shark.

These gentle giants have a very specialized way of feeding. As they swim, they suck up great gulps of ocean water, a bit like an enormous underwater vacuum cleaner. The water passes through a filter, which sieves out any bits that are good to eat, before being pushed out through the whale shark's incredible gills.

Whale sharks are found in tropical waters all over the world, often venturing quite close to the shore. Measuring up to 40 feet in length, they can grow as long as a bus and weigh as much as four elephants!

Like many other sharks, whale sharks are caught and killed by humans for their meat and fins. Sometimes just the fin is removed and the rest of the shark is thrown back into the water. This cruel practice is illegal across most of the world but sadly still happens in international waters.

Because of their large size and slow pace, whale sharks can also be hit by boats and propellers and are sometimes caught in large nets that have been put out to catch other fish, such as tuna.

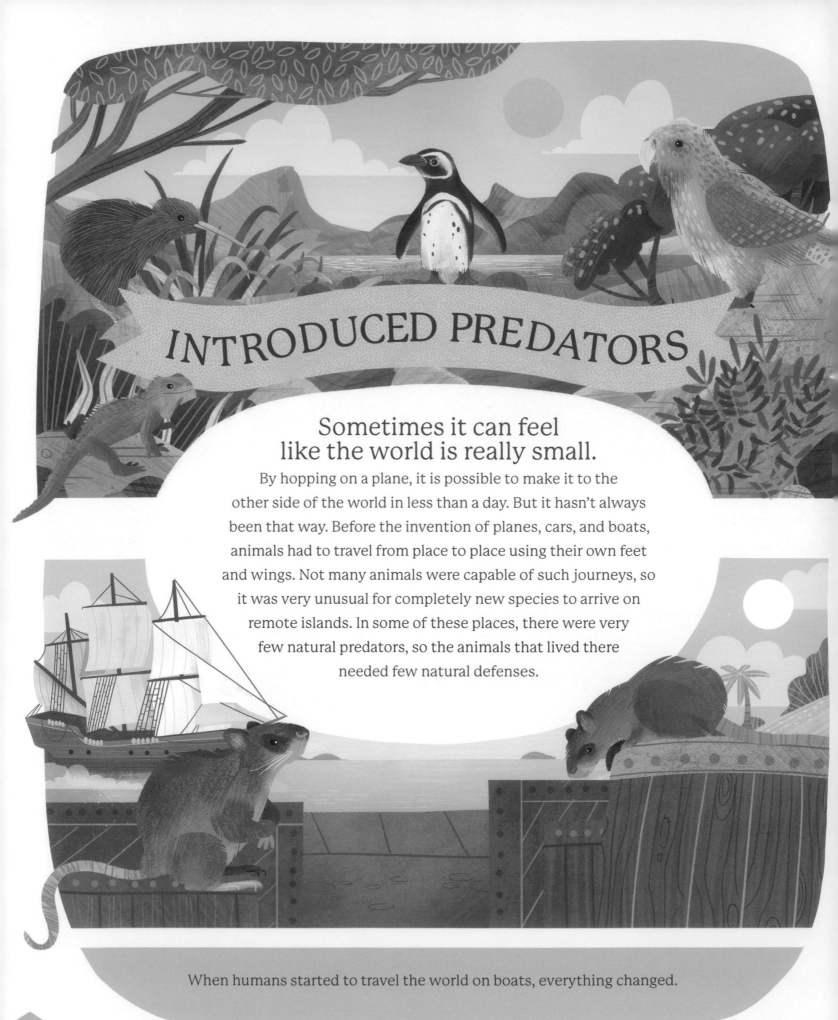

INTRODUCED PREDATORS

Sometimes it can feel like the world is really small.

By hopping on a plane, it is possible to make it to the other side of the world in less than a day. But it hasn't always been that way. Before the invention of planes, cars, and boats, animals had to travel from place to place using their own feet and wings. Not many animals were capable of such journeys, so it was very unusual for completely new species to arrive on remote islands. In some of these places, there were very few natural predators, so the animals that lived there needed few natural defenses.

When humans started to travel the world on boats, everything changed.

Rats and mice traveled on the ships of the first explorers. Rats ate the eggs and chicks of many birds which nested on the ground, who were not used to hiding their babies away.

Cats and stoats were released on purpose to control the numbers of rabbits and rodents. They are excellent hunters and killed many birds and bats too. Hundreds of species are directly threatened by cats.

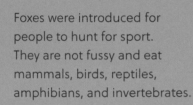

Foxes were introduced for people to hunt for sport. They are not fussy and eat mammals, birds, reptiles, amphibians, and invertebrates.

Cane toads were released in Australia to eat grubs that were munching on the sugar cane plantations. They are packed with poison that makes them deadly to any larger animals that eat them.

Farm animals such as pigs and goats were brought over to farm for meat. Many of these escaped and cause great damage to ecosystems.

The effect of releasing these animals into new environments was devastating. Hundreds of species were wiped out forever and many more continue to be threatened.

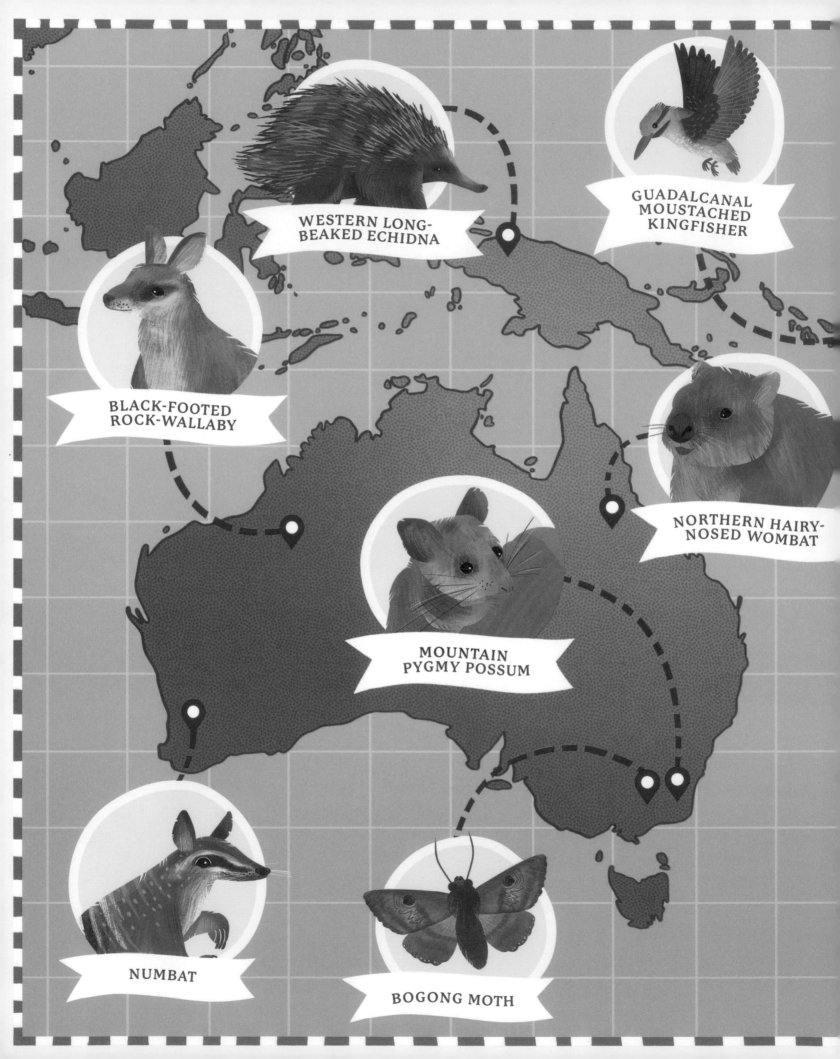

WESTERN LONG-BEAKED ECHIDNA

GUADALCANAL MOUSTACHED KINGFISHER

BLACK-FOOTED ROCK-WALLABY

NORTHERN HAIRY-NOSED WOMBAT

MOUNTAIN PYGMY POSSUM

NUMBAT

BOGONG MOTH

OCEANIA

LAU BANDED IGUANA

TAKAHĒ

The islands of Oceania are home to all kinds of weird and wonderful animals. Most of the mammals here are marsupials—animals that carry their babies in pouches—which are very different from the mammals found in the rest of the world. The birds here are different too: many of them live on the ground and cannot fly. Lots of the unusual creatures that live in Oceania are not found anywhere else on Earth.

Oceania is made up of much more ocean than land, making it impossible for many animals to travel between the islands.

KĀKĀPŌ

Australia is an enormous island, with lots of different habitats, from hot and steamy rainforests to cool freshwater lakes. In the center of Australia there is a vast, dry area known as the outback. Australia's animals are uniquely specialized to thrive in these habitats, so it is very important that we protect them.

Kiwis are pretty noisy. They use a combination of snuffles and grunts to communicate and have even been known to purr!

Catlike whiskers

Kiwis have nostrils at the end of their beaks, allowing them to sniff out grubs and earthworms and gobble them up in the dark.

53. Kiwi

Technically, kiwis are birds. They have beaks, feathers, and wings. But for all the similarities they share with birds, plenty of things about the kiwi are downright *odd* too. Their feathers are soft and silky, more like shaggy hair than feathers. Their bones are full of marrow, making them squat and heavy—unlike most birds, which have hollow bones so they are light enough to take to the air. Kiwis are so unusual among birds that some scientists call them "honorary mammals."

But why have kiwis ended up this way? At the time kiwis were evolving, the only mammals in New Zealand were bats. As kiwis did not need wings to escape from predators, they became adapted to life on the ground. Their wings got smaller and smaller and their legs grew thicker and stronger. As there were no mammals on the ground, snuffling about for insects and waddling around in the dark, kiwis filled this role instead. Eventually, the kiwi came to be more like a badger or a hedgehog than an eagle or a sparrow.

Kiwis lay enormous eggs! One kiwi egg can weigh up to a quarter of the weight of an adult kiwi.

Unfortunately, mammals *were* eventually introduced to New Zealand—and kiwis were not equipped to escape them. As a result, kiwis were frequently killed and injured by dogs, ferrets, and stoats. Now we know how dangerous mammals can be to kiwis, conservationists have set up kiwi-safe zones, where kiwis can live and lay their eggs in safety. Hopefully this will be enough to save this peculiar flightless bird—and it will be waddling around New Zealand for many more centuries to come.

54. Black-footed rock-wallaby

The quick and nimble black-footed rock-wallaby is perfectly adapted to the rugged landscapes of central and western Australia. Its flexible cushioned paws allow it to move easily across steep and craggy rocks and its long and powerful tail helps it to balance. Black-footed rock-wallabies are very shy and will bound quickly away from any sign of danger. These agile gymnasts were once common across Australia's mountainous regions but are now only found in small and isolated populations.

55. Northern quoll

Under the cover of darkness, northern quolls prowl the forests in search of small animals. These cat-sized marsupials can be aggressive hunters but will feed on just about any food they find—as long as it's meat! Unfortunately, when poisonous cane toads were brought to Australia, they became a prime snack for northern quolls. Over time, the cane toads' toxic flesh resulted in many northern quoll deaths. Now northern quolls only survive in isolated areas, mostly in rocky uplands.

56. Mountain pygmy possum

It's easy to miss mountain pygmy possums since they like to tuck themselves away in cracks and crevices. In fact, they are so good at hiding that we once thought they had gone extinct! It was quite a surprise when one was spotted at a ski lodge in Victoria, Australia, in 1966. Now there are around 2,000 mountain pygmy possums left, hidden high up in the mountains.

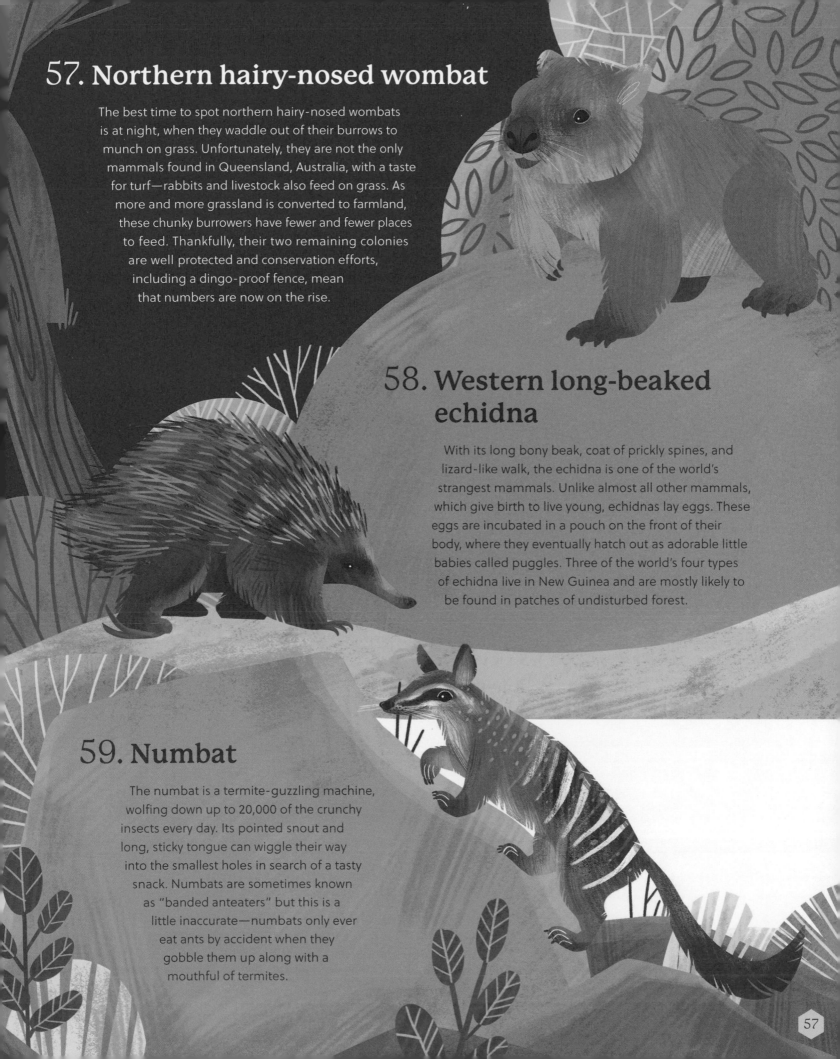

57. Northern hairy-nosed wombat

The best time to spot northern hairy-nosed wombats is at night, when they waddle out of their burrows to munch on grass. Unfortunately, they are not the only mammals found in Queensland, Australia, with a taste for turf—rabbits and livestock also feed on grass. As more and more grassland is converted to farmland, these chunky burrowers have fewer and fewer places to feed. Thankfully, their two remaining colonies are well protected and conservation efforts, including a dingo-proof fence, mean that numbers are now on the rise.

58. Western long-beaked echidna

With its long bony beak, coat of prickly spines, and lizard-like walk, the echidna is one of the world's strangest mammals. Unlike almost all other mammals, which give birth to live young, echidnas lay eggs. These eggs are incubated in a pouch on the front of their body, where they eventually hatch out as adorable little babies called puggles. Three of the world's four types of echidna live in New Guinea and are mostly likely to be found in patches of undisturbed forest.

59. Numbat

The numbat is a termite-guzzling machine, wolfing down up to 20,000 of the crunchy insects every day. Its pointed snout and long, sticky tongue can wiggle their way into the smallest holes in search of a tasty snack. Numbats are sometimes known as "banded anteaters" but this is a little inaccurate—numbats only ever eat ants by accident when they gobble them up along with a mouthful of termites.

60. Guadalcanal moustached kingfisher

Ko-ko ko! Somewhere in the mossy Guadalcanal forest in the Solomon Islands a Guadalcanal moustached kingfisher is calling. Known by locals as the Mbarikuku, the spectacular Guadalcanal moustached kingfisher cannot be found anywhere else in the world. Despite its showy plumage, it mostly prefers to remain out of the limelight, tucked away in the treeline or safely hidden in its burrow.

61. Takahē

For fifty years, the brightly colored, turkey-sized Takahē was no more than a memory. People marveled at stuffed Takahē in museums across the world, remarking sadly that the bird was now extinct. But one man did not believe that the Takahē were gone. In 1948, a doctor named Geoffrey Orbell set out on an expedition to the remote Murchison mountains, convinced that he would find Takahē hiding there—and he was right! Now, the remaining Takahē are fiercely protected and their numbers continue to grow.

62. Kākāpō

Parrots are all bright, multicolored birds that live in the Amazon rainforest, right? Wrong! Bumbling through the undergrowth of island forests in New Zealand, the kākāpō is a large, nocturnal, flightless parrot, whose feathery sideburns make it look more like an owl. Critically endangered, the kākāpō now only survives in a handful of protected areas, away from introduced mammals.

63. Tasmanian devil

A snarling wail rings out into the black night of the Australian island of Tasmania, and a dark, shadowy figure bursts into view. It is black and cat-sized, like a large rodent or a very small bear. This is the Tasmanian devil! It has bright, inquisitive eyes and a curious, twitching nose—constantly on the lookout for food. Primarily scavengers, Tasmanian devils are not fussy and will eat just about any animal they come across, using their powerful jaws to chomp their way through every last bite of the carcass—even the bones!

64. Lau banded iguana

Lau banded iguanas spend most of their lives in the trees, lounging lazily in the Fijian sun, searching for leaves and flowers to eat, or watching over their territories. Males are very territorial—if they spot another iguana wandering into their patch, they will rush over to defend their home, aggressively bobbing their heads and lunging toward the intruding male.

65. Dugong

Taking life in the slow lane, dugongs are peaceful marine mammals that spend their days bobbing around in warm coastal waters from Africa to Australia. Bristly, sensitive snouts and strong flexible lips help them to tear up tasty seagrass, which is how they spend most of their days.

66. Bogong moth

If you were a moth, living in Queensland, Australia, where would you go on your summer vacation? Well, if you were a bogong moth, you would probably go to a small cave or crevice in the mountains of Victoria, where you would remain huddled, with thousands of other bogong moths, for several months, before flying back to Queensland to breed and lay your eggs. What an adventure!

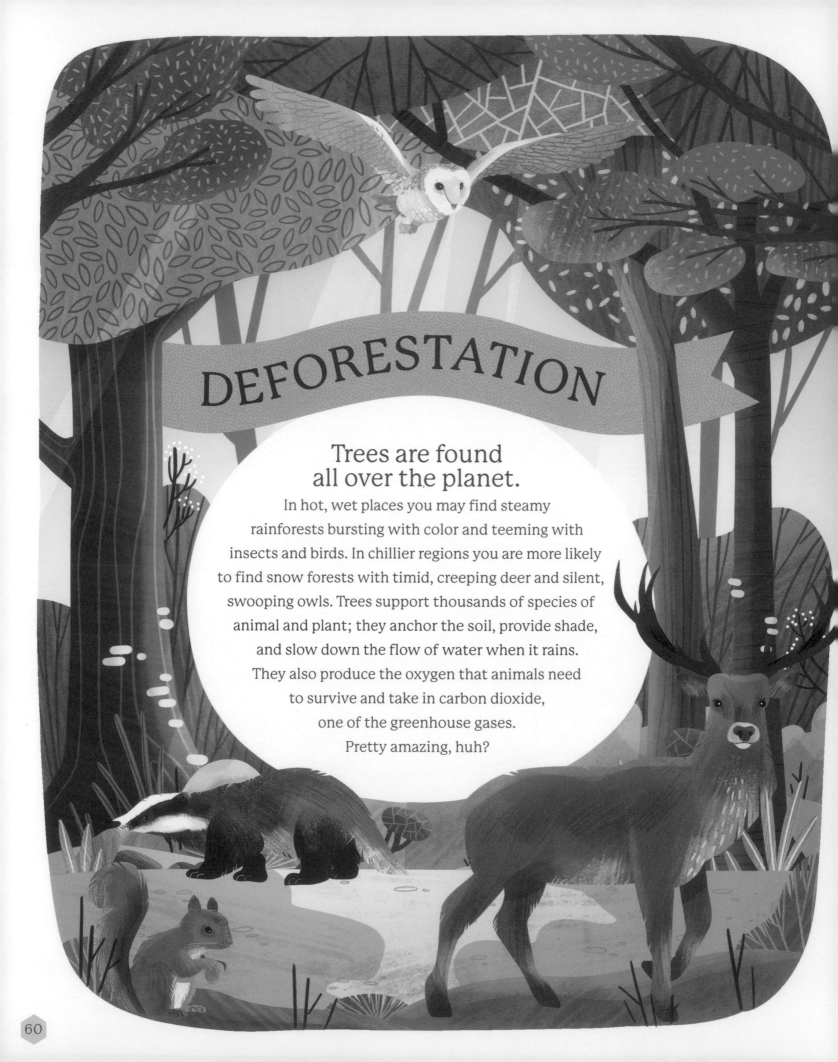

DEFORESTATION

Trees are found all over the planet.

In hot, wet places you may find steamy rainforests bursting with color and teeming with insects and birds. In chillier regions you are more likely to find snow forests with timid, creeping deer and silent, swooping owls. Trees support thousands of species of animal and plant; they anchor the soil, provide shade, and slow down the flow of water when it rains. They also produce the oxygen that animals need to survive and take in carbon dioxide, one of the greenhouse gases.

Pretty amazing, huh?

Though the Earth's forests are all very different, they share one thing in common: they are threatened by humans. Sometimes we clear forests because we want to use the land for something else instead, such as farmland or a settlement. We also make things from cut down trees, such as paper or furniture. Wood is also used as a fuel. Whenever trees are cut down, animals suffer.

When we lose trees, animals lose their homes, which is desperately sad, but that's not the only way our planet suffers. If we cut down too many trees, we stop our planet from being able to protect itself against global warming, flooding, landslides, and droughts.

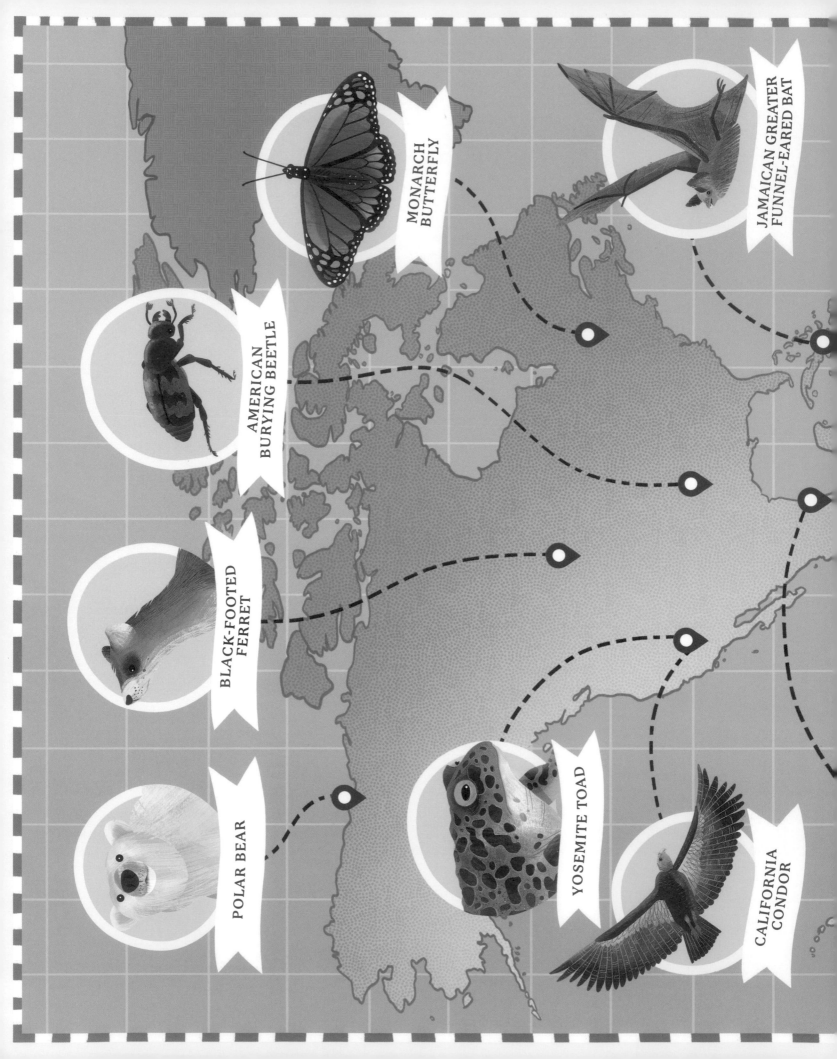

MONARCH BUTTERFLY

JAMAICAN GREATER FUNNEL-EARED BAT

AMERICAN BURYING BEETLE

BLACK-FOOTED FERRET

POLAR BEAR

YOSEMITE TOAD

CALIFORNIA CONDOR

GIANT OTTER

HUEMUL

WHITE-BELLIED
SPIDER MONKEY

GALÁPAGOS
SEA LION

AXOLOTL

AMERICAS

The geography of the Americas forms a kind of frozen sandwich, with the tundra of Alaska and the glaciers of Patagonia as the icy bread at either end. In the middle, all manner of extraordinary habitats can be found, including scorching deserts, rolling grasslands, sweltering jungles, sprawling cities, and breathtaking mountains.

From the bright lights of the big city to the wide-open grasslands of the Great Plains, North America's varied environments provide homes for a colossal array of incredible animals.

The Americas are home to some of the world's most extraordinary wetlands, including the Pantanal, the world's largest flooded grassland, and Lake Titicaca, the world's highest lake.

South America is home to the world's largest rainforest, the Amazon. This gigantic forest covers nine countries and more than 40% of South America. It is home to more species of plants, birds, mammals, reptiles, amphibians, freshwater fish, and insects than anywhere else in the world. It is also home to around 30 million people.

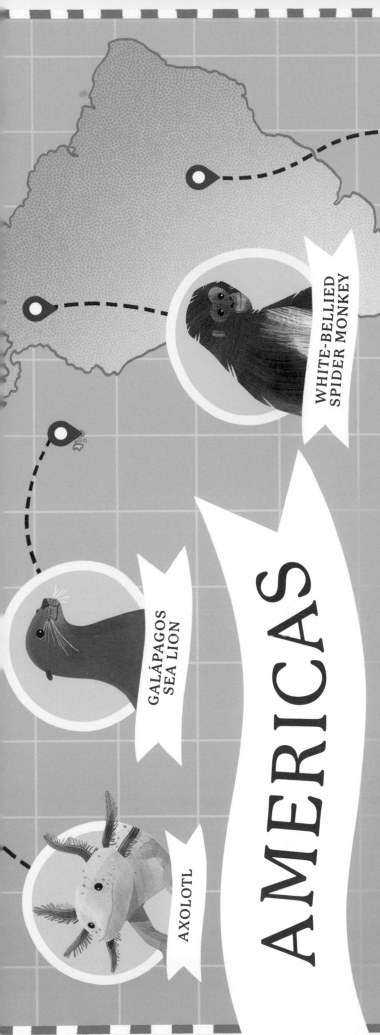

67. California condor

Few birds are as impressive in flight as the magnificent California condor. Its enormous wings stretch 10 feet across, and it can soar on thermal currents at speeds of up to 55 miles. California condors keep the wilderness clean by feeding on the carcasses of large dead animals. In the past, this habit was their downfall because they were often poisoned by lead bullets, but a successful conservation program has helped California condor numbers to recover and today they continue to rise.

68. Polar bear

The northern polar regions are ruled by polar bears. These giant carnivores are supremely adapted for life at the top of the Arctic food chain, feeding mostly on seals, which they hunt off the edge of sea ice. While their unique adaptations are perfect for life in the icy cold, polar bears would struggle to live anywhere else. If temperatures continue to rise, there is a chance that we could lose polar bears completely.

69. Darwin's frog

Darwin's frog is one of the animal kingdom's most devoted dads. Unlike any other known amphibian, he will take the eggs into his mouth and store them in his vocal sac. Protected inside his body, the eggs grow into tadpoles and then froglets. When they are old enough to take care of themselves, their father will spit them out again.

70. Monarch butterfly

In a cloud of orange, a flurry of monarch butterflies descend on a sacred fir tree. These extraordinary insects have traveled 3,000 miles to spend the winter in Mexico, after living in Canada and the northern US for the summer. Millions of monarch butterflies currently make this migration every year but rising global temperatures threaten to change that—as temperature increases can have devastating effects on milkweed, the plant that monarch caterpillars rely on to survive.

71. Jamaican greater funnel-eared bat

My, what big ears Jamaican funnel-eared bats have! All the better for pinpointing flying insects in midair. They are expert fliers, using ultrasound to map their surroundings and zipping easily through dense plant growth in pursuit of their prey. Like other funnel-eared bats, they roost in caves, but the Jamaican funnel-eared bat is now only found in one cave and there are fewer than 100 individuals left.

72. Black-footed ferret

It was a huge surprise when a sheepdog named Shep discovered a black-footed ferret on a Wyoming ranch in 1981. Before that, people had believed the black-footed ferret was extinct. After a good search, eighteen black-footed ferrets were found and taken into captivity so that they could breed. Now there are more than 300 black-footed ferrets in the wild, all descended from the original eighteen. Well done, Shep!

73. Yosemite toad

With its sheer granite rock faces, plunging waterfalls, and towering sequoia trees, Yosemite National Park in the western USA is a true natural wonder. It is a haven for wildlife, home to bears, coyotes, and bobcats, as well as countless birds, fish, and insects. With such incredible scenery to see, it can be hard to tear your eyes away and look down at the ground, but you will be rewarded if you do! The wet mountain meadows throughout Sierra Nevada are bursting with rare plants and animals, such as Yosemite bog-orchids and Yosemite toads.

Yosemite toads are never far away from a water source, often hatching out in pools of melted ice water or swimming around as tadpoles in slow-moving mountain streams. In the hot, dry months, Yosemite toads will seek out moisture wherever they can and will often be found under rocks and logs, or even sheltering in cattle hoofprints!

Yosemite toads are disappearing across their range. They face many threats, including conversion of their habitat to farmland, poisoning of their streams, and collisions with cars.

During the breeding season, noisy male Yosemite toads are sometimes mistaken for birds!

At night, Yosemite toads bury themselves in soil or find themselves a cozy rodent hole to hide in. They hibernate for the coldest months of the year.

74. White-bellied spider monkey

White-bellied spider monkeys are the unwitting gardeners of tropical rainforests across northern South America. Using their long arms and powerful tails to swing through the trees, they are experts at finding tasty forest fruits. After guzzling their tropical fruit feast, white-bellied spider monkeys move onto a new site, where they drop the fruit's seeds—wrapped in a handy parcel of fertilizing poop—which can then grow into new plants.

75. Giant otter

Like a huge, hairy fish, the giant otter glides gracefully through the rivers and creeks of the Amazon basin. Biggest of all the otters, it can reach over six feet in length—so it's not surprising that it is known as "river wolf" across much of its range. Giant otters are excellent swimmers, using their powerful tails and webbed feet to speed through the water, searching for tasty fish to eat.

76. Galápagos sea lion

The unique animals of the Galápagos Islands are some of the most interesting creatures on Earth. They famously inspired Charles Darwin's theory of evolution and still attract thousands of visitors every year. Galápagos sea lions are one of the most commonly seen mammals on the islands. They are playful and curious and are often seen swimming in the shallows or galloping around on the shore.

77. Huemul

Chile's national mammal, the huemul, is a critically endangered deer found in the mountains and fjords of Argentina and Chile. Huemuls are very hardy and can survive in very cold conditions—sometimes even living next to enormous glaciers! Huemuls are excellent swimmers and can often be spotted far off the shore of Patagonian lakes.

78. American burying beetle

The super-sensing American burying beetle uses its highly sensitive feelers to sniff out dead meat and can detect a dead body that is miles away. Most active at night, once an American burying beetle arrives at a carcass, it busies itself burying the body. The dead meat will act as an incubator for the eggs and a food source for the babies once they hatch.

79. Axolotl

Imagine a tadpole that—instead of turning into a frog—got bigger and bigger but didn't change its body shape at all. That's exactly what happens in the strange case of the axolotl. Salamanders usually start their lives in the water, just like tadpoles, then transform into creatures that live on land. But instead of following the usual rules, axolotls remain in their baby form forever, growing in size until they are around a foot in length.

80. Devil's Hole pupfish

Death Valley in California is so hot the air feels like it has come directly from a hairdryer. Only specially adapted animals can live in these conditions—animals like the world's rarest fish, the Devil's Hole pupfish. These small blue fish live in the hot and salty waters of Devil's Hole, a water-filled limestone cavern in the middle of the Amargosa Desert.

ANIMALS NEED OUR HELP

The decisions we make every day have an impact on animals all over the world,

so it is important to make choices that have a positive impact, things like walking instead of taking the car or trying to produce less waste. There are also things we can do to support the animals who live in your local area.

Creating a wild space in your garden or at your school is a great way to support local wildlife. It doesn't need to be big! You could try:

CREATING A BUCKET POND OUT OF AN OLD WATERTIGHT CONTAINER

Remember to place stones at the bottom for insects to shelter in and a stick against the edge to help animals climb in and out. Fill with water and pond plants then wait to be amazed at how many pond creatures find their way to their new home!

PUT UP A BAT OR BIRD BOX

Bat and bird boxes are a great way to encourage wildlife into your yard, but make sure to do some research about where to put them. They must be somewhere safe from predators like squirrels and cats, sheltered from the weather, high enough from the ground to allow a clear flight path in and out, and not too close to bird feeders or other nest boxes.

LEAVE A MESSY CORNER

Clean and tidy yards are a disaster for wildlife, so why not choose one corner to leave in a mess! A pile of rotting logs makes a perfect shelter for a hibernating hedgehog or a snoozy snake, while piles of old bricks make perfect homes for insects and lizards.

PLANTING A NECTAR GARDEN

Throw down some seed and grow a patch of nectar-rich native flowers to keep the insects in your area fueled up while they are busy pollinating. Try to pick varieties that flower in different seasons, so that hungry pollinators have something to eat year-round. If you have enough space, adding in shrubs that produce tasty berries can provide a great place for birds and mice to rest. If you're especially lucky, they may even stay to make a nest!

INDEX